The Purple Cow

by Liza Charlesworth

ISBN: 978-1-338-29810-9
Illustrated by Jenn Harney
Art Director: Tannaz Fassihi; Designer: Michelle H. Kim

10 9 8 7   68   20 21 22 23 24/0
Printed in Jiaxing, China. First printing, June 2018.

2

5

7

8

12

14

15

16

Gus Gumball

by Liza Charlesworth

ISBN: 978-1-338-29811-6
Illustrated by Jenn Harney
Art Director: Tannaz Fassihi; Designer: Michelle H. Kim

10 9 8 7   68   20 21 22 23 24/0
Printed in Jiaxing, China. First printing, June 2018.

■ SCHOLASTIC

4

9

13

14

15

F

Scary Things

by Liza Charlesworth

ISBN: 978-1-338-29809-3
Illustrated by Jenn Harney
Art Director: Tannaz Fassihi; Designer: Michelle H. Kim

10 9 8 7   68   20 21 22 23 24/0
Printed in Jiaxing, China. First printing, June 2018.

3

4

5

7

9

13

14

15

16

The Slow Race

by Liza Charlesworth

ISBN: 978-1-338-29812-3
Illustrated by Jenn Harney
Art Director: Tannaz Fassihi; Designer: Michelle H. Kim

Copyright © 2018 by Liza Charlesworth. All rights reserved. Published by Scholastic Inc.

10 9 8 7   68   20 21 22 23 24/0

Printed in Jiaxing, China. First printing, June 2018.

3

6

7

12

14

15

Hello!
I am Worm.
I go slow, too.
Can I race you?

Rose and Daisy

by Liza Charlesworth

ISBN: 978-1-338-29813-0
Illustrated by Jenn Harney
Art Director: Tannaz Fassihi; Designer: Michelle H. Kim
Copyright © 2018 by Liza Charlesworth. All rights reserved. Published by Scholastic Inc.
10 9 8 7   68   20 21 22 23 24/0
Printed in Jiaxing, China. First printing, June 2018.

SCHOLASTIC

5

9

10

15

The Class Clown

by Liza Charlesworth

ISBN: 978-1-338-29814-7

Illustrated by Jenn Harney

Art Director: Tannaz Fassihi; Designer: Michelle H. Kim

Copyright © 2018 by Liza Charlesworth. All rights reserved. Published by Scholastic Inc.

10 9 8 7   68   20 21 22 23 24/0

Printed in Jiaxing, China. First printing, June 2018.

3

Everyone thinks I am funny but Sam.

7

10

Oh, no!
The mouse crawls
into my shirt.

11

Hey, that tickles!
I wiggle and giggle.
I run all around.

12

13

Pigerella

by Liza Charlesworth

ISBN: 978-1-338-29815-4
Illustrated by Jenn Harney
Art Director: Tannaz Fassihi; Designer: Michelle H. Kim
Copyright © 2018 by Liza Charlesworth. All rights reserved. Published by Scholastic Inc.
10 9 8 7   68   20 21 22 23 24/0
Printed in Jiaxing, China. First printing, June 2018.

5

7

9

10

13

15

And the two pigs oinked happily every after.

F

Rock, Paper, Scissors

by Liza Charlesworth

ISBN: 978-1-338-29816-1
Illustrated by Jenn Harney
Art Director: Tannaz Fassihi; Designer: Michelle H. Kim
Copyright © 2018 by Liza Charlesworth. All rights reserved. Published by Scholastic Inc.
10 9 8 7   68   20 21 22 23 24/0
Printed in Jiaxing, China. First printing, June 2018.

3

4

6

7

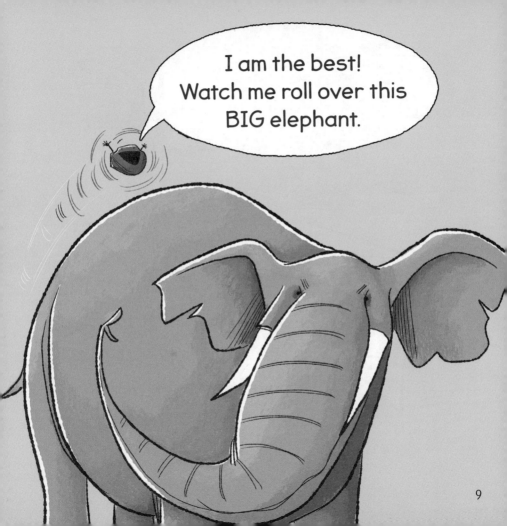

9

Dear Rock, Paper,
and Scissors,

You are ALL
the best!

Love,
Pen

#1

14

15

The Gloves

by Liza Charlesworth

ISBN: 978-1-338-29803-1
Illustrated by Eric Barclay
Art Director: Tannaz Fassihi; Designer: Michelle H. Kim
Copyright © 2018 by Liza Charlesworth. All rights reserved. Published by Scholastic Inc.
10 9 8 7   68   20 21 22 23 24/0
Printed in Jiaxing, China. First printing, June 2018.

2

4

5

9

10

13

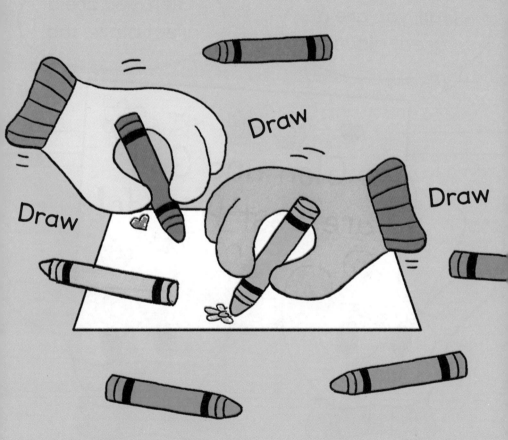

15

Meg and the Moon

by Liza Charlesworth

ISBN: 978-1-338-29806-2
Illustrated by Eric Barclay
Art Director: Tannaz Fassihi; Designer: Michelle H. Kim
Copyright © 2018 by Liza Charlesworth. All rights reserved. Published by Scholastic Inc.

10 9 8 7   68   20 21 22 23 24/0

Printed in Jiaxing, China. First printing, June 2018.

SCHOLASTIC

5

7

9

13

14

15

Pete and Polly

by Liza Charlesworth

ISBN: 978-1-338-29804-8
Illustrated by Eric Barclay
Art Director: Tannaz Fassihi; Designer: Michelle H. Kim
Copyright © 2018 by Liza Charlesworth. All rights reserved. Published by Scholastic Inc.
10 9 8 7   68   20 21 22 23 24/0
Printed in Jiaxing, China. First printing, June 2018.

3

4

7

9

11

12

13

14

Goldimouse

by Liza Charlesworth

ISBN: 978-1-338-29801-7
Illustrated by Eric Barclay
Art Director: Tannaz Fassihi; Designer: Michelle H. Kim
Copyright © 2018 by Liza Charlesworth. All rights reserved. Published by Scholastic Inc.
10 9 8 7   68   20 21 22 23 24/0
Printed in Jiaxing, China. First printing, June 2018.

5

7

8

9

11

13

15

16

Mad Cap

by Liza Charlesworth

ISBN: 978-1-338-29802-4
Illustrated by Eric Barclay
Art Director: Tannaz Fassihi; Designer: Michelle H. Kim
Copyright © 2018 by Liza Charlesworth. All rights reserved. Published by Scholastic Inc.

10 9 8 7   68   20 21 22 23 24/0

Printed in Jiaxing, China. First printing, June 2018.

4

9

12

14

15

16

The Big Baby

by Liza Charlesworth

ISBN: 978-1-338-29805-5
Illustrated by Eric Barclay
Art Director: Tannaz Fassihi; Designer: Michelle H. Kim
Copyright © 2018 by Liza Charlesworth. All rights reserved. Published by Scholastic Inc.
10 9 8 7   68   20 21 22 23 24/0
Printed in Jiaxing, China. First printing, June 2018.

2

7

9

11

15

The Shape Snake

by Liza Charlesworth

ISBN: 978-1-338-29807-9
Illustrated by Eric Barclay
Art Director: Tannaz Fassihi; Designer: Michelle H. Kim

10 9 8 7   68   20 21 22 23 24/0
Printed in Jiaxing, China. First printing, June 2018.

3

5

11

13

14

15

The Three Little Snowmen

by Liza Charlesworth

ISBN: 978-1-338-29808-6
Illustrated by Eric Barclay
Art Director: Tannaz Fassihi; Designer: Michelle H. Kim
Copyright © 2018 by Liza Charlesworth. All rights reserved. Published by Scholastic Inc.
10 9 8 7   68   20 21 22 23 24/0
Printed in Jiaxing, China. First printing, June 2018.

SCHOLASTIC

2

4

5

7

9

11

13

14

15